The Ridings

Emma Conally-Barklem

To Raquel, with much love & good wishes! Emma xxx

First published in Great Britain by Bent Key Publishing, 2023
Copyright © Emma Conally-Barklem, 2023
The moral right of the author has been asserted.

All rights reserved. No part of this book may be reproduced in any form or by any electronic or mechanical means, including information storage and retrieval systems, without permission in writing from the publisher, except by reviewers, who may quote brief passages in a review.

About the Author photo © Dr Zuzana Bajuszova. Cover photography © Emma Conally-Barklem.

ISBN: 978-1-915320-26-1

Bent Key Publishing
Office 2, Unit 5 Palatine Industrial Estate
Causeway Avenue
Warrington WA4 6QQ
bentkeypublishing.co.uk

Edited by Rebecca Kenny @ Bent Key
Cover art © Samantha Sanderson-Marshall @ SMASH Design and Illustration
smashdesigns.co.uk

Printed in the UK by Mixam UK Ltd.

*I have ridden the waves of grief and will keep riding in your memory.
This collection is for you, dear mum; I miss you.*

Kathleen Anne Conally

1953-2018

And for my dad, maybe we'll always walk those moors together

Clifton Conally

1953-2023

Praise for *The Ridings*

With its title denoting the three ancient counties of Yorkshire, this is a collection very much rooted in place, identity and a sense of belonging. There is a pride that comes with the language of growing up in a 1980s working class family; this is presented effectively using list forms sometimes interspersed with a voice in Yorkshire dialect who becomes a comedic commentator on the action, and dialogue with multiple speakers. This all makes for a pleasingly varied collection in its style and presentation.

But when counties are marked there is division, and The Ridings explores this theme with powerfully-expressed personal experience. There is also the connotation of riding out the storm, surviving a difficult time, and in Conally-Barklem's case, grieving the death of her beloved mother.

Skilfully crafted, poignant and memorable, this is an impressive debut which I am sure will be of great comfort and inspiration to anyone experiencing loss.

Natalie Scott, Poet

The Ridings by Emma Conally-Barklem was written "during the dark years of the pandemic", in the wake of her mothers' death, and is described by the poet as "both a personal reckoning with self and grief as well as a re-imagining of the Yorkshire folk [she] grew up with".

Those folk are working class, both first-gen immigrant and born & bred, and this chapbook is alive with their idiosyncrasies of dialect, comfort food, commemorative knick-knacks and respectable attitudes. Here is the familiar clutter of life, made precious by careful poetic cataloguing. Grief and missing sound their notes throughout, but it isn't a constant clamour...

...Yorkshire itself inhabits this book, which can be no bad thing (as well we know, it's God's Own Country). Time after time, the poet and the poems roam back to the landscape, where trees and rocks are carved with dates long past their significance, by human hands long-gone.

Kirsten Luckins, Poet

Contents

Preface	vii
Lodged In My Throat	11
Best Things Past Their Best	12
Paternoster Lane	13
A Meteor Landed on Baildon Moor	14
Working Class Pudding	15
Don't forget where you came from but know you can never go back / If the cap fits	17
If Anyone Asks!	18
Care Home	19
Give Us a Twirl!	20
Vine Terrace (East)	22
Clothes on the Line	23
No Coward Soul Am I	24
Mágoa	25
Evie Grace	27
cis	28
Hiraya	31
motes float	33
Lovers' Beech / Aborglyph	35
Bad Linen	36
When I'm Not Around	37
8/08/88	38
Home Fires	39
Acknowledgements / About the author	41
Notes	47
About Bent Key	48

A sweet taste of Yorkshire... nostalgic references to the past transport you into a field of your own memories. Emma's poetry has a way of gripping your heart and guiding you down the paths of her experiences as if she is walking with you.

Sharena Lee Satti, Poet

Preface

This collection was written between 2020 and 2022 during the dark years of the pandemic and during a period of self-reflection, processing, honouring and therapy, except for *Care Home* which was written over twenty years ago.

Maybe I was always a poet. Sometimes we meet our selves further down the line and say, "Oh yes, I remember you!" Sometimes it takes something monumental to push us into our home self where the ghosts stare and face them down. For me, this was the death of my precious mother. She nurtured my reading and writing with trips to Bradford Central library; she always said I should write more but I kept it hidden. I started writing for her as she could no longer, and then gradually for myself, and then gradually for us both.

The Ridings is both a personal reckoning with self and grief as well as a re-imagining of the Yorkshire folk I grew up with. Some home-grown, some first-generation immigrants from Jamaica. Idiosyncratic, funny, mysterious and generous, as only working-class folk are. The title comes from an old gilt-framed map my parents had on the landing stairs which showed The Ridings of Yorkshire. I ran up the stairs two at a time past this map for many years before I left for university. I came to look at it as an adult and found it was gone like so many things which slip through complacent fingers.

The landscape of West Yorkshire beats inside memory: bleak, obtuse, life-affirming and now on these pages.

The Ridings

Lodged In My Throat

Lodged in my throat; is it a sticky willow or is it a conker?
Spiky.
Shot down at the age of 5 and festering ever since,
No rinse can clear it.
Instead, the child curled inside the wardrobe must be allowed her time.
Daisies held, hopeful to reclaim what is hers and mine.
Before trauma trailed her dusky skirts across her heart line.
A voice, bell-like, to announce truth as our identities intertwine.

Best Things Past Their Best
for Roy, Shirley, Winnie and Cherry

This room is for best!
All our best things go in here —
Best table, best ornaments, dumb waiter, tea service, Princess
    Diana commemoration plate, carved wood from The Homeland,
    drinks trolley, macramé doilies
Are held in aspic
Plastic covers everything
So if you sit, you squeak.
The roiled patterned carpet appears in mustard & brown swirls
    as if from a Northern pier arcade
You teeter your way through to the loo past all the best things.

A whiff of curried goat, spiced rum cannot penetrate this stunned
    lair
Us like Bisto kids, eyes big, noses lifted in the air

Have a care! This space is a cut above
We're in Yorkshire now love, where our sovereign's son passed
    through,
Prince Charles visited Wool Combers Mill,
A vinyl Union Jack waved from a brown wrist, cold nose in
    anaemic sun.

So,
Just in case,
Think. On.

Someday, someone else will come, deign to visit,
Deserving of all this finery in this stone-slabbed terrace
A tryst or afternoon tea sipping with someone deserving of royalty.
Until then, keep off!
'Cos this room's for best!

Paternoster Lane

I smear our names, *Mum and Emma*, in the grimy glass, sitting atop
   the double-decker
A treat to sit at the front on a school day.
Off sick, mum takes the day and here we are, travelling
A stop at Paternoster Lane to say, 'Ahhhh!' and have my arm
   squeezed uncomfortably tightly
You sit, reassuring, handbag full to bursting, brolly soggy with the
   perpetual rain of winter.
A diversion; the bakers for some treats for the poorly, a day where I
   have you to myself.

My small hand in yours as we get sprayed by the traffic and
   shrug off steaming coats, get cosy by the gas fire.
Kettle on, my picture books and your magazines, day time TV
   and tea as the pale sun moves from window to window,
   winnowing time which stretches endlessly when you're young.
A mum lasts forever, a warmth to snuggle into, cuts tended, bruises
   soothed, a heart to bleed into.
All is ordinary 'til now,
When your absence fills my hollows
With an ache I'm not used to.

A Meteor Landed on Baildon Moor

After the Cinder Rock on Baildon Moor, Bradford, West Yorkshire, which to my childish eyes looked like a meteor. My father carried me to see it on his shoulders before a degenerative disease robbed him of his ability to walk

A meteor landed on Baildon Moor
A cinder seed head set in Betelgeuse fronds
Huge wand of pumice lost in a bath of bee-parsed heather,
Crass, mithered with hidden rabbit holes.

As dusk approached, I bobbled on his shoulders,
Small hands cleaved his coal wound curls
As he strode out, effortless, in post-work enthusiasm towards the devilled worsted rock.

She, scurrying besides with soda pop & tissues
Eyes lined up with horizon & brined with West Yorkshire bristling

A trig point stop-off, panorama as the moors loomed & shattered for light years.
Placed down, crescent moon fingernail picks at glitzy mica & porous tooth
A flashy medallion on flaxen breast of sheep sorrel & acid grassland.

Sienna sky & clinker heaps, man's detritus from mining but lining the core of our *Star Man* minds
Is a Jet jewel dropt
Black star liner
Shipley comet
Lugged out from the cosmos,
Spacewalk before his legs were held hostage.

Working Class Pudding

Semolina, Sago, Treacle Sponge
Angel Delight, Rice Pudding, Arctic Roll,
& Jam Roly Poly?

It's cold outside
Yer need a bite
After bangers n' mash
Or corned beef hash
There it is
In crystal form
A magic dish
Of milk n' bits
Add butter, sugar & jam
Better than *Spam*!
Frog spawn or sago
To put you on
After *Bullseye* & pie
Chipped pots
Proper scran
Ambrosia rice if yer posh
Failing that
An *Angel Delight*!
In butterscotch, strawberry
Chocolate or lemon
Dished out in *glass*!
Oooh no, it's too cold for that love!
Cold outside? ...on a Shipley night?
Just boil a fizzin' tin o' treacle
Birds Eye custard, lumps n' skin

By eck, it's roastin!
Now then:

Arctic roll by the slice
That's nice!

It doesn't jar me teeth!
Champion!
I ad a reet good feast!

Don't forget where you came from but know you can never go back / If the cap fits...

I come from miners' terraces / Cows by a river / Farmers n' shopkeepers / Chip butties / Hot patties / Pardoners, loan sharks n' catalogue payments / Becks, snickets n' ginnels / Chimneys n' white sands beaches / Lino, flock wallpaper n' dropped glass bottles / Flat vowels n' patois / Daily Mirror & The Gleanor / Ringtons tea & ice cream soda / Forerunners n' bystanders / Malham n' Kingston / Mediums n' reggae artists / Red Stripe n' Tetley's / Desmond's n' Coronation St / Tanned hides n' belt licks / Well... if the cap fits

If Anyone Asks!

If anyone asks, say tha's from Leeds, not Bradford!
Like the Harry Enfield sketch:

Sophistication? Sophistication??
Don't talk to me about sophistication, av bin to Leeds!

A cut above, six miles down the M62 is a dilettante's paradise:
The Calls, the halls of commerce, Wall's ice cream van, ham by the
    slice in Rawson's Market.

Hell's bells, av bin missing out!
So if in doubt, deny thrice St George's Hall, the Alhambra, Imax
    camera,
Writ in red — Leeds is my true homestead.

Care Home

work hurt today; voice screaming, static crackling
lips drying
almost dying,
shelled people
in their chairs,
stared out from a deep place
uninhabited
purple, bruised
and paper in my hands
a breeze to knock them flying
and me
paid
paper
to help them on their way

Give Us a Twirl!

Like the Swan Lake ballerina in her indigo box
That sings silvered notes and aloneness,
I pirouette on beige lino, which is meat-spattered & curling

A space demarcated, spotlight down
for the male gaze
Those of the father-protector
So the message is confused

Usually I, truculent & combative,
Would say, 'Go to hell!'
But now:
Cowed brown girl at a tea dance,
Meek, obliging like a Regency heroine

She, with eyes ice flecked, turns a slow infinity to tinkled bells in
   tulle tutu
Swan Lake theme that turns me to tears even now, a gift from the
   absent mother.
Did she turn like this, in secret photographs to titillate?
Did she dream her way out of an indigo box to escape this
   tinselled Sisyphean fate?

Now, in the kitchen that smells of bacon fat and stale cigarettes
   — shall I prance?

Each time I enter, is she thinner or fatter?

Feistiness dissolves in the cattle handler's appraisal, where my
hide is never quite smooth

Give us a twirl!

So I can observe the areas which fill you with shame
Battle lines drawn on the abdomen

Turn around so I can see you!

Pronounce judgement in the complacent air of a man for whom
    every woman is fair game.
Stranger at a bar, wife, Miss World, daughter

Let's watch; we'll watch together
With notepad, the Daily Mirror & pen
To score these women as they parade, gloss angular & jutting

But don't we all seek world peace?
Freed from this scene of overhead lighting & stifled desire

A hurried freshen-up in the car
Lipstick & eyeshadow, a bra back on at the turn of a key
Perfume sprayed, until the pieces line up, a centrifuge in reverse

And I can spin like Lynda Carter, your pin up, ready for the
    greeting:

Right, let's have a look at you!

Now

Hair free from chemicals, face free from cosmetics, body free from turning, mind free from misogynistic influence, now, see, spy, the truths housed inside me where your gaze cannot reach.

Vine Terrace (East)
for Winnie & Charles Hiley, my grandparents

You can tell a lot about folk by their curtains,
She said.
Pinny on, up at dawn, marching with 'Mad Lizzy'.

Barm cake for dinner with Potted Dog.
Glance out again, eyes agog:

She's late up, and what's he lakin' at?
The neighbours don't cut the mustard.
Let her sen go!
Laddered tights a broken web steeped in defeat.
Feverish scrubbing: a whitened doorstep bulwark against such sartorial disaster.

That collar needs a wesh!
Daylight bends around net curtains.
Charlie's off out, muffled leave-taking; *See a man about a dog.*
Bit o' peace, cup of Rington's tea *avec saucer.*

Hayley Mills in Whistle Down the Wind
Just resting me eyes 'til Countdown
Cutlets and mash, steamed windows, ironing fug.
Shirts marshalled, collars scrubbed, job done.

It's only me Grandma!
Hello Love!

Returning prodigal, nicks Parma Violets from chest drawer
Turns a blind eye,
Bigger fish to fry in this Bradford terrace, back to back,
Cheek by jowl,
Thick as thieves, lives
Stacked around
Routine.

Clothes on the Line

Push them aside 'cos they block the sun.
Let's raise our faces
like tulips, feel rays bathe us
on the kitchen step.

Wind swishes briefs & jeans,
In lethargic Tarantella
this heart-line now severed,

Your clothes dispassionate remains of the time we spent
Sunbathing,
Carefree, lazing, between clothes on the line.

No Coward Soul Am I

A knock at the classroom door, morning fugue of teenagers, teacher filled with caffeine-optimism and love of the Brontës.

No, this isn't African Studies, starched pause, lambent air of embarrassment as woke students snigger, *Jeez Miss, really?*

I mean really?

Did I hear clearly?

Incredulous swallowed-back shock, swearing solidarity from cynical white youth, the truth of this racism archaic as chalk on board.

He really did say that, but there's no such thing on the syllabus, so was he just taking the piss or trying to dismiss my right to educate in the ways of literature,

Histrionic female mulatto has no rights here, in the hallowed halls of Shakespeare, did you think education would clear, the decks for respect?

I continue, defiant as Emily knowing the remedy is me imperious, brim full of books and passion, no rash reaction, instead going higher, words as swords,

So, fall back anachronistic tutor, as I sally forth into a new future.

Mágoa

A longing for a home or feeling which no longer exists (Spanish)

I washed up today on the tideline of your handbag
Two purses
One for everyday use
One for holidays and days out
Receipt for our Afternoon Tea, January 2018
Train ticket to York for a hotel stay.

Picked up your glasses
                    The glass fell out
I was incensed, as if someone had poked a finger in your eye
Hair (synthetic) in a zipped freezer bag (undated)

60 Euros for Portugal, Bureau de Exchange receipt, folded and
    faded.
I scale for skin cells.

Hold glasses delicately aloft
Glint in the weak October sunlight,
I spy   fingerprints
Whorls of unique truth
Semaphore of a being, irreplaceable, no fingers exist
But here you are offering me Monopoly money when I can't travel

Though, I think of boarding a plane where my name is my only
    currency and the meteor-clump of molten ache will be hand
    luggage (undeclared)
An M&S lipstick (unused)
Pencil written list:
Aprons, bread, toothbrush (underlined), Fairy (Liquid not sprite)

I sit now, on the kitchen windowsill
Clear away the unidentified herb plant carcass that still remains
The grubby leavings you'd have cleared.

Perch above as you wash dishes, absent-minded

We can sit (simultaneously)
I can hand you your handbag of
Purses, photos, receipts, glasses, lipstick, list, a pen saying *Sister*, tickets, mobile phone (dead), driving license, store cards, coach card, Emergency Care card, Gold Line patient card

Minus the last two
As if they didn't exist

Just the usual mum stuff in this battered bag
So you can look indignant, wondering how it ended up in my hands
Why I look so lined, broken, now relieved, grateful
Knowing as you gather me in for a casual cuddle (though for me it's been so long)
I'll have to hold back, act normal, hold on to you and this illusion lest the bag is all that remains.

Evie Grace

She holds us all in the weight of her soul
Arch curved like an ammonite, shelled, the air is static
Keighley-clean in a triple team who cleave the air as if fingers
   were wings,
She the jewel in the diadem,
Glancing blows, she moulds wheels to mantras, at a canter,
   springs through May
Evie Grace makes shapes with her namesake

cis

1

I'll just piss out here then, shall I?
Make your life easier
Then you need never chime, *I think you're in the wrong toilet!*
According to what, may I ask?

a) My appearance b) your confident judgement of my gender c) your sense of male and female according to your own socialisation d) your sense of how the world should operate e) your comfort zone f) your right as the self-satisfied majority to step into my business?

All answers to be recorded, systemised, ratified.
And, if I am non-binary, in transition — what then?
Should I go in the Gents and then the Ladies to even things out, 50/50 or
I'll just piss out here then, shall I?
Or, maybe I should crawl back to the edges of existence where
    you don't need to think about me.
Only 1% of us, so best forgotten.

2

unbound,
a prototype,
blueprint of how to live fearlessly, ceasing to transmit a chimera incarnation of a hologram self.

Why should I tiptoe, cringe and explain my actions to you?
1% of us here who wish to mother, teach, cradle and hold but you have to be human to do that and somehow the labels accumulate, papier-mache binding of print, Times Roman, wrap around a around a human soul 'til choked you give me no option than to go

plural they/them so I can gather the selves you negate and deride, there is power in numbers, to blow a hole through the conceit that little boxes can hold us.

And this is all... to walk undetected without recrimination.

He felt, **she** felt this pronoun trap

3

every time I visit a railway station rest room, as you walk in nonchalant, I wait for your eyes to alight on me and see the difference, indistinct but there,
you frame your words and I hunch, slink with trepidation and defiance as you give the lie to my right to be in this grimy stop-off when all I want is to enter careless and complacent like you
marooned in the behemoths of **HE** and **SHE, GENTS, LADIES** , essentialistic semaphores, archaic as a doily,
                                        the complacency of being **cis**,
where your face fits and no-one debates whether you have the right biology to enter and wee without challenge, simmering hostility

fear of **the other** as you've been designated in antiquarian chests which hold truth and absolutes.
Protected from hate by law but what of insidious side-eye judgements, bulwarks and pillars challenging my existence, revulsion pouring off their shoulders, sulphurous, a mustard gas miasma of fear WHICH STINGS me — not them.

4

She wanted to teach, the courage it took to go ahead and find the truth of herself beyond the assumptions of colleagues and friends.

shoe-horned identity when all they felt was an urgent proclivity to align. No, a hunger, a need to be seen as me, appreciated in the totality of me-ness.
You whittle and reduce so it behoves me to stand my ground
'Cos ones will come after
More vulnerable, filled with self-loathing, more doubtful, be scarred by this hidden discrimination
then maybe, finally things will change.

5

A rest room's a rest room,
we all do the same,
we bleed the same ,
the forms will change,
why does my gender,
my orientation matter in the workplace,
for the online course,
for entering this gym?

Don't you see the intimidation — where sometimes it is best to stay home, away from unrealistic expectations, where my doors are not labelled and my dog sees me through love's eyes.

6

'Cos ones will come after, on the train shoulder blades bristle with self-awareness
Stepping now, through darkened door,
Rustle of shopping bags,
Taint of urine to the olfactory, there you are
Mighty of voice and opinion,
I slice through, intent on my business,
Which you have no part of.

Hiraya

Hiraya (tagalog)
Hi-ra-ya

Hiraya, taken from an ancient Filipino word meaning the "fruit of one's hopes, dreams, and aspirations", originates from the popular phrase "Hiraya Manawari," which generally means, "may the wishes of your heart be granted".

These thought patterns are like rail tracks with no
Branch
lines.
We can't see our way out of our reality which is to prize haircuts
   and holidays over more hearts beating.

The seating is close, lest we get too cold from distance from one
   another.

Our compassion extends as far as a handclap or rainbow, crude
   but sincere in a window.

Not to the people working shifts as they move in prickly animal
   concentration of sweat and worry,

      a slow asphyxiation
            in a mask
                  to keep you safe

Whilst we traipse around bars, inhibitions discarded as hands
   circle lampposts and carouse.

No dots to join here.
You are working hard and we need a beer.
Never the twain will meet.
Parallel lines, a child's face pressed to glass, steaming frustration
   at grandad's incarceration in Care,

Where we discharge aerosols and motes into frail hearts which don't stand a chance.

How can your uncle's death relate to my night out?

We take safety measures which bend to our own plans, because liberty, being British is important.
Don't take my liberties, or tell me what to do! Who the hell are you to tell me how to live my life?

It's just figures on a screen, nothing to do with me, probably massaged and manipulated like the scientists simplified metaphors for the deplorable reality we don't want to face.
Moon shots and mountains to climb?

Give me a break,
    we know the news is Fake.

A number could be a man who refused an ambulance, breathless but fine really; *Man Flu,*
I'll come up in a few weeks, just getting over this cold
Now lays in a hallway, fraught neighbour couldn't penetrate his bastion of denial and now a daughter weeps, come too late as she corrugates herself with falsified guilt.

His poems and documents silt up the windows.
An artist's death re-visited; not starving in a garret but prone on patterned carpet 'til the cops kick the door in.
Stone dead.
Another number, tucked underneath the lino.
Something out of nothing.

motes float

motes float   motes float
(imperceptible but inhaled)
            how far do motes float?
              (ocular debris, exhale dust)

in a tower block
in a packed theatre
in an outdoor festival
from my dentist's mouth
from the man jamming his trolley into my backside cos im
    dressed for an asbestos factory
(rubber-lipped fish goggles keep flotsam particles away)
gloves double mask   goggles
(close to the shoals shutters down pratyaharic unknowing)

i dont care,
    dont care what you think,
        what you think about bleaching the walls cos the snows
  too bright on a snow day
i dont care,
    dont care what you think
        what you think about hoovering a yard cos the bits
  congeal in corners
(spews out more particles than it sucks in dont look)

walk past my window and laugh at my hijinks   madcap
                                  love&light u
                                        p
                                        s
                                        i
                                        d
                                        e
                                            down
on a yoga mat

(crumbs & hair unsettle my zen-like stare)

dont mock me or sneer cos I dont care whatyouthink inablink

cos this dust builds an a v a l a n c h e inside me

and
now

motes float   motes float

(and breath is no longer my friend)

Lovers' Beech / Aborglyph

Character my love upon the tender tree trunks they will grow, and you, my love, grow with them
Eclogues of Virgil

You host secret initials on private land,
R.S, F.S
The year 1956.
Words on board a bark of common beech.
Masthead, figurehead, vision quest for canopy,
Uncommon traceries of intimate connection.

Lovers' Beech, lone totem, towering past to best lost love.
A pen, a knife, a sharp etch into history,
Tender words brave the saw-toothed edges,
Echoed couplings hush sylvatica hymn through oval leaves

Aborglyph, a semaphore of our love.
Sinuous sojourn through the ventricles of a multi-stemmed heart,
Letters bulge into hieroglyphs, carried up;
Amorphous, alluring,
The sun sap of passion bright,
Light dexterous fingers now stilled by time.

Bad Linen

Inspired by a painful memory of a visit to my mum before she died and Michel Faber's poem for his wife who died of cancer, Such a Simple Thing I Could Have Fixed *in* Undying: A Love Story

On dad's side of the bed, it needed changing, creased & stained, a
  rectangle of broderie anglais around cotton from the seventies.
Long overdue, an air of neglect, a room imbued with Complan &
  ashy, stale tea.

Mum, I came here, past the blood on the wall, past the human
  traces,
To see the spaces where you used to be,
Now, sad creature inert like paper, and he, blithe & denying the
  state of things.

Could it be any sadder? Could it?
Be any sadder to see bad linen dashed with flecks of blood and
  Complan

Sad that I come only now as you shrivelled to the toxic mass of all
  that shady medicine.

Pillowcases, antimacassars carry human traces, the soil is left but
  all I saw was neglect

So I changed it, held your dense-pain head in the bowl of my
  suntanned hand & exchanged bad linen for good.

When I'm Not Around
for Uncle Michael

For a brief time in August, he was a genius.
His Anansi-like scrawls, celluloid walls, a tipped-out mandala of
   chaotic paving

They eulogised, inveigled truth, sighed, frying in Methodist pious
   heat;
Mumbled words of his from foolscap, words that would never hit
   his face, laced with admiration   guilt a gild-edged evocation
Of the love they *FELT*

Which washed clear, somehow, of his life, mysterious lone
   creator eluding convention in the theatre of his mind,
kind Jesco prophesised the horror of the times his childhood
   dreaming couldn't handle
The schemers, shooters, swindlers, vandals tore down his
   barriers to the Infinite:
Holding a chariot of wolds & snickets, ginnels, fricative cricket
   chirrups the destiny of those who stand free

Words... their liberty

8/08/88

My heart travels across moor and heath
To a distant rock etched with the date 8/08/88,
Where we'll walk damson heather and scree, eternally

Silken Ilkey's sylvan hills
bitter turf & falling rock
the gargle of brook
bronzed pebble waters
pale denim
Benson's cigarette
Sit for sarnies & juice

Just us on this rock of moor
Barren but lush
Sunday's hush
of no people

Immortalised moment
fingers mould the year
lichen scraped away
scurrying spider
We were here

Four raw born of chimneys & farms
heart-sore with bills & pollution
a white wells absolution

Distilled smooth rabbit's skull
bones to step over

You'll see this date at some distant time
when drones exist
and know
we were here

Home Fires

This peat was used to heat homes, burnt turf, steaming of long dead creatures, heather root and loam.

I feel a longing for these walks, sharp crisp air and soft water, your skin luminescent, tinged red with cold. Our laughter choked back by vicious blast which must have frozen the sisters' feet fast to the earth, tender as unfledged birds.

Our memories fluting upwards in a baleful Yorkshire sky, scalding tea a remedy for all ills, our hearth tilled by rain and bluster.

We shelter in near Top Withins, eyes filled to brim with strange primal beauty emitted to only those who see their souls reflected indifferently in curlew's call and waterfall,

An imperfect homecoming, now, as I walk alone, bereft, windswept towards the moors

Which shape shift under cumulous cloud, tumulus hills marked ordinance, space to grieve and hold a hardy wildflower close, tiny bells of hope chime nature's song, though you are gone.

Acknowledgements

First, a huge thank you to Rebecca Kenny & Bent Key Publishing for accepting 'Vine Terrace (East)' with warmth & gusto followed by my chapbook. Thank you for acknowledging, welcoming, and creating a home for raw, vulnerable writing and championing working class writers. I will be forever grateful and proud to be part of the Bent Key fam: weirdos, misfits, talented luminaries unite!

Thank you to the online writing community for your encouragement, support, and inspiring work. Thanks to Sharena Lee Sati, Kirsten Luckins, Bryan Dunne for hosting me and Kristiana Reed for supporting my work from the start. A huge thank you to Sassy Holmes for helping me realise a dream and the Brontë Parsonage Museum for supporting my fusion of poetry with wellbeing and to the many writers and poets I have connected with.

Secondly, I would like to thank the folk of God's Own County including the Conally, Terrelonge and Hiley families, and the beautiful, bleak landscape which infuses this collection. Yorkshire born and proud.

Thank you to Sam for bringing your unique and dazzling talent to the design of the collection and Lorna for supplying precious images of family past which provide the backdrop to this collection.

Thank you to my dear Yorkshire grandma Winnie for helping shape who I am today, my grandad Charles as well as my Jamaican grandparents Louis and Rosa, your influence runs through these pages.

To the forerunners lost before and in the writing of this collection: Dean, Michael, Winnie, Cherry, Roy and to the friends found

Marie, Anna, Kas, Cynthia, Vish, Pen, Sabrina, Michelle, Jo, Manj, Helen, Mandy, your support at a difficult time will never be forgotten.

Thank you to the Bajuszova family for your endless generosity and taking me in to your chaotic, loving family.

To Mama Alica, thank you for being a mother to me when I really needed one.

To Zuzana, for your unconditional love, always supporting everything I do and being with me all the way through this emotional rollercoaster of a collection. I love you.

Lastly, to my dear funny, creative, kind and beautiful mother, Everything I write is for you and always will be. I hope I make you proud. Love from Gerbie.

About the Author

Photo: Dr Zuzana Bajuszova

Emma Conally-Barklem is a yogi, writer and poet based in North Yorkshire, England. She writes on nature, mental health, grief, social justice, family and wellbeing. Her poetry has been published in *Free Verse Revolution* Literary Magazine, *Please See Me Online* Literary Journal, *Aurum* Journal, *Poetic Reveries* Magazine, Sunday Mornings at The River, *Ey Up!* Bent Key Publishing Anthology of Northern Poetry 2022, *Tipping the Scales* Literary Journal, Small Leaf Press, *Super Present* Magazine, West Trestle Review, QuillKeepers Press, Querencia Press, *Wild Roof* Journal, *Last Stanza Poetry* Journal, Black Cat Poetry Press and *In Her Space* Journal.

Pushcart Prize-nominated Emma had a summer residency at the Brontë Parsonage Museum and was named one of Ilkley Poetry Festival's New Northern Poets 2022. Her yoga and grief memoir, *You Can't Hug a Butterfly: Love, Loss & Yoga* will be published in 2024.

Find her work online at www.emmaliveyoga.com and on IG @emmaliveyoga.

Notes

'Lodged in my Throat' first published in Winter Issue #9 2021 *Please See Me Online* Literary Journal

'Give Us a Twirl!' first published in *Cassandra:* Issue V *Free Verse Revolution* Literary Magazine

'Lovers' Beech/ Aborglyph' first published in *Trees, Seas & Attitude* Anthology, Black Cat Poetry Press, 2023

'Vine Terrace (East)' first published in *Ey Up: An Anthology of Northern Poetry,* Bent Key Publishing, 2022

'No Coward Soul Am I' first published in *Black in White* Community Collection Anthology

'Home Fires' first published in *Hestia (hearth & home)* Issue III, *Free Verse Revolution* Literary Magazine

About Bent Key

It started with a key.

Bent Key is named after the bent front-door key that Rebecca Kenny found in her pocket after arriving home from hospital following her car crash. It is a symbol — of change, new starts, risk, and taking a chance on the unknown.

Bent Key is a micropublisher with ethics. We do not charge for submissions, we do not charge to publish and we make space for writers who may struggle to access traditional publishing houses, specifically writers who are neuro-divergent or otherwise marginalised. We never ask anyone to write for free, and we like to champion authentic voices.

All of our beautiful covers are designed by our graphic designer Sam at SMASH Illustration, a graphic design company based in Southport, Merseyside.

Find us online:
bentkeypublishing.co.uk

Instagram & Facebook   @bentkeypublishing
Twitter   @bentkeypublish